WHERE IS JESUS NOW . . .
AND WHAT IS HE DOING?

Front cover picture:

Dinah Kendall is a personal friend of the author and readily gave permission for one of her pictures to be used for the cover. Her fascinating style, not unlike Stanley Spencer or Beryl Cook, brings the gospel events up to date in a striking way, using local scenes (in this case the stable yard where she lives). She also shares with the author a conviction that the world of art can and must be captured for Christ and used for the glory of God.

Where Is Jesus Now...

and What Is He Doing?

J DAVID PAWSON MA, BSc

KINGSWAY PUBLICATIONS
EASTBOURNE

First published 2001

ISBN 0 85476 930 7

Published by
KINGSWAY PUBLICATIONS
Lottbridge Drove, Eastbourne, BN23 6NT, England.
E-mail: books@kingsway.co.uk

Designed and produced for the publishers by
Bookprint Creative Services, P.O. Box 827, BN21 3YJ, England.
Printed in Great Britain.

Contents

1

What Is the 'Ascension'?

Jesus came into this world and went out of it in a different way from everybody else. Both his arrival and his departure were quite unique.

He had no human father, either within or outside a marriage bond. His mother was a virgin throughout the conception, pregnancy and delivery. There have been a few other such claims. If confirmed, they would be examples of the spontaneous division of a female egg without fertilisation, a process familiar in the plant and animal world and known as parthenogenesis. But in the human species it could only produce baby girls. And Mary had a boy. Only the almighty Maker of heaven and earth could have made that possible.

Even more astonishing, Jesus claimed to have chosen to be born! His repeated statements about his life's purpose always began with: 'I came'. Furthermore, he said he had come down from heaven to earth.

This descent is usually referred to as his 'incarnation' (literally: 'in-flesh-ing'). It was not just a move from heaven to earth; it was also a change of existence from the divine to the human – or rather, from being God to becoming a God-man. The Son of God was now the Son of man. For the first time he had a physical body. He was a human being, just like us.

Thirty-three years later he returned to where he'd come from. He went back up from earth to heaven. Christians call this his 'ascension'. They believe in a Christ who has both descended and ascended (Ephesians 4:9–10).

They have not coined a corresponding yet contrasting word to 'incarnation' (like 'excarnation', for example, literally: 'out-flesh-ing'), for a simple yet vital reason. When he went back to heaven he did not cease to be a man. He did not leave his humanity behind, just as he had not left his divinity behind when he came.

His departure was also unparalleled. Others leave this world on the day they die; he stayed around for two more months. Others leave this world because they are dead; he left very much alive. Others leave their bodies behind; he took his with him.

Neither Jesus' incarnation nor his ascension is central to the Christian faith. Neither is found in all four Gospels or is prominent in the Epistles. His crucifixion and resurrection take the place of 'first importance' (1 Corinthians 15:3–4). Yet whenever fundamental Christian beliefs have been listed in the basic, brief statements called 'creeds' (the 'Apostles'' and 'Nicene' being the best known and most widely used), his dying and rising have been set between his being born and his ascending. They provide the essential context within which he accomplished all he came to do. Without coming to us and going from us, he could not have saved us from our sins. We would still be struggling with them – and losing the battle.

Along with creeds, many churches have developed a

calendar to embody these fundamentals of the faith in annual festivals. Easter celebrates the cross and the empty tomb, since both happened at the Jewish spring feast of Passover. Christmas celebrates the birth, though the date of December 25th belongs to a pagan midwinter rite welcoming the re-born sun. Both are widely observed, even by non-Christians (who see them as holidays rather than holy days).

By contrast, Ascension Day (40 days after Easter Sunday) passes by almost unnoticed. I went to a school that gave us a holiday on that day, provided we attended a service at a nearby cathedral (I never understood what it was all about). A few churches hold a communion service on that day (I still don't understand why recalling Jesus' crucifixion is an appropriate way to celebrate his ascension). But for the most part, this key event in the life of our Lord is totally ignored, especially by those churches sitting lightly to traditions, including the ecclesiastical 'year'.

Why this neglect? Why does Jesus' coming into the world create such interest, even excitement, while his going from it is treated with apathy and indifference? Why are there so few books about it (and even they do not become bestsellers)? There must be a reason.

2

Why Is It so Neglected?

The ascension has been described as 'the Cinderella of the creed'. She was the neglected, even despised, member of the family. Her existence was acknowledged, even her usefulness. But she was simply not taken into account when important matters were discussed.

Perhaps this comparison is a little harsh, but there is truth in it. The lack of thoughtfulness is common to both. Reader, be encouraged. In picking up this book, you have begun to think about this most neglected part of our faith in Jesus.

But why has the ascension been so overlooked? Many reasons have been suggested, from the simple to the profound. Let's look at some of them.

First, Ascension Day is celebrated on a Thursday. If it had been on a Sunday, when Christians are together for worship, perhaps more notice would have been taken – as with Easter Sunday, for example. But this is not an adequate explanation. Christmas can fall on any day of the week, and the crucifixion is remembered on Good Friday (actually, Jesus probably died on a Wednesday, the following day being a 'special Sabbath', not Saturday: John 19:31). Christians turn out in large numbers on these weekdays, no doubt encouraged by their status as national holidays. It is hard to avoid the conclusion that they don't consider the ascension that important to their salvation. The same applies to the next suggestion.

Second, the ascension has not been linked to nature. Christmas has been linked to midwinter and Easter to spring, associating the ecclesiastical with the natural calendar, giving more 'meaning' to the celebrations. However, it needs to be pointed out that this only applies in the northern hemisphere and leads to ludicrous anomalies in the southern (cotton wool 'snow' stuck on Australian shop windows at the height of summer, for example). And Pentecost (Whit Sunday), though originally connected to Israel's harvest time, has no agricultural significance now, yet draws considerable attention.

Third, we are more moved by Jesus' coming to us than his going from us. We are always more glad to say hello than goodbye. Separations are sad. Is, then, the real reason for our neglect of the ascension emotional? Are we so man-centred and earth-centred that we can rejoice over his coming among us (remembering that 'Immanuel' means 'God with us'), but grieve over his going from us? Those who leave this world tend to become irrelevant and forgotten unless directly related to us. Are we subconsciously resisting this happening to our Lord? Is that why we celebrate his arrival more than anyone else's and neglect his departure more than anyone else's? It is an intriguing psychological theory – but probably too subtle and therefore unlikely, certainly as the basic reason.

Fourth, we have simply not understood its importance. We are not quite sure how it fits into 'the way' of salvation. This is particularly true of Western Christendom. Since the big split of 1054, churches in the West (both Catholic and Protestant) have put the death of Christ on the cross at the centre of their preaching (and often their architecture). Eastern (Orthodox) churches have focused their gospel on the resurrection, which seems nearer to the apostolic proclamations recorded in the book of Acts. This difference of emphasis on the dying or rising Christ can have a direct effect on our thinking about him. In the one case we concentrate on what he did for us in the past, whereas in the other we find ourselves meditating on what he is doing for us in the present and *where* he is doing it. One sees the resurrection as the essential sequel to the crucifixion; the other sees the ascension as the essential sequel to the resurrection.

Preachers and teachers must take the blame for this failure to grasp the full sequence of 'salvation-history', as scholars call it. Few work systematically through the creeds. Even fewer regularly expound and explain the New Testament passages relating the event. Fewer still take the trouble to show why Jesus *had* to remove himself if he was to complete his work for us. There has been an added complication, particularly among 'evangelical' Christians. Pastors and evangelists have so stressed Jesus living in our hearts that many believers tend to think of him as still on earth, rather than back in heaven, seated at the right hand of God his Father. (See Chapter 9 for a fuller look at this misunderstanding.)

So there is unlearning as well as learning to do, if the ascension is to regain its proper place. This publication has been written precisely to aid this re-education. But before we can get on with it, we need to face another explanation that has been put forward, which underlies both the objections of unbelievers and the hesitations of believers in this modern age.

Fifth, the story of the ascension is simply not considered

credible in this scientific age. In the light of our increased knowledge of the universe and the way it works (our 'cosmology'), the notion of someone going up from earth to heaven is unbelievable, if not impossible.

This 'problem' is so widespread, even within the church, that we must devote a whole chapter to the question: 'Where is heaven?'

3

Where Is Heaven?

It must have been easier to believe in the ascension when people thought the earth was flat. Heaven was 'up above' and hell was 'down below'. Anyone going from earth to heaven would go straight up into the sky.

Today, all but a few obscurantists have a very different view of the universe and the place of our planet within it. 'Up into heaven' has been replaced by 'out into space'.

The earth is not flat, with edges off which sailing ships could fall. It is a sphere, round which ships and now planes, even space capsules, can travel. It is also revolving on its own axis.

Since Copernicus' discovery that the earth goes round the sun, not vice versa, and the more recent realisation that the whole universe is a gigantic sphere expanding with increasing speed since the 'big bang' that started it all off, our thinking has undergone a radical revolution.

If heaven is beyond this physical universe, it is an inconceivable distance away. If it is within our universe, whereabouts is it? With all bodies revolving as they do, a vertical line based on the Mount of Olives could point anywhere at all.

So where did Jesus go when he 'ascended to heaven'? Scripture traces his departure as far as his disappearance in the clouds, but no further. Where was his ultimate destination? Where is he now?

Such questions may not trouble simple Christians who don't think much about their faith. They sincerely read the Scriptures and recite the creeds without facing the issues raised, accepting what is contained there in simple faith. But this attitude is inadequate when commending the gospel to others in this modern age. Unbelievers expect a valid belief system to fit the world as we know it and make sense of it.

A whole new generation has grown up in the 'space age', with a totally different perspective, vividly expressed in photographs of the earth 'rising' above the moon's horizon. Radio telescopes have examined distant stars as well as 'hearing' the sun. Probes have reached every planet in our solar system. Above all, human beings have visited space, stayed there for a time and even plan to live there in the future. Are they nearer to heaven the further they go from earth?

It might be thought that the advent of astronauts would have made it easier to believe that a man called Jesus 'ascended to heaven'. On the contrary, the idea is not less but more offensive, since such a trip is 'impossible' without a powerful rocket to free from gravity, a spacesuit to protect from solar hazards, a means of propulsion and a life-support system. In fact, no modern man has actually been 'in' space; he can only survive in a cocoon of earth's environment. A returning American astronaut, asked if he'd met God up there, replied: 'No, but I would have done if I'd taken my spacesuit off!' Jesus didn't have one on.

Let us admit that there are real difficulties, both here and in other parts of the Bible, which appear to run counter to 'scientific' opinion. Informed readers of Scripture are aware of such 'problems', especially if they are also enthusiastic evangelists seeking to commend the Christian faith to their contemporaries. They find themselves fulfilling the task of 'apologetics', an unfortunate term suggesting they are embarrassed by or even ashamed of their beliefs. Actually, it refers to the need to offer reasons for their hope, explaining how it fits the facts of our existence, showing that believing does not involve intellectual suicide. Faith goes beyond reason, but not against it. 'Truth' and 'reality' are the same word in both the Hebrew language of the Old Testament and the Greek of the New.

One way of resolving the tension between science and Scripture is increasingly popular, even among Bible scholars. That is to treat problem passages as 'myth'. That does not mean that such narratives are untrue; only that they are a different kind of truth. Not literally, physically or historically true; but morally, psychologically or spiritually true. They give us *values* rather than facts. They are stories with a message. Aesop's fables are a good example; they are 'true to life', even though they never actually happened. Such fiction can communicate Christian truth. The allegory of Bunyan's *Pilgrim's Progress* comes to mind. Jesus' own parables are surely such imaginative constructions intended to make a point.

Though there clearly are some 'myths' in our Bible, there is an alarming tendency to extend this category to cover any narrative presenting difficulties to the modern mind, regardless of content or context. Beginning with such 'stories' as Adam and Eve in the garden and Jonah in the whale, it has gradually spread from the Old to the New Testament, to the 'miracle stories' in the Gospels and even the resurrection of Jesus.

The ascension has not escaped. The 'story' is said to embody the values of the disciples' faith in Jesus, rather than any facts about his bodily departure from them. The 'tale' expresses their belief that he is of higher status than anyone else who has lived on earth; it is their way of saying: 'We will always look up to him; he is above everyone else in our opinion.' So it is said that they made up the story of his ascension to give their conviction a concrete rather than an abstract form, knowing that 'all the world loves a story' and will remember it much more easily, when it is not merely verbal but able to be visualised. To communicate its truth today, it is argued that the myth needs to be 'demythologised' by concentrating on the truth it contains, not the 'fictional' framework in which it is set.

Though this relieves the science-versus-Scripture tension at a stroke, it does so at great cost. Christianity is a historical faith, depending on facts, not fiction. If Christ was not raised from the dead, the Christian faith is worse than useless, a dangerous delusion, the greatest fraud in history, having fooled millions. The same applies to the other literal facts, historical events summed up, for example, in the Apostles' Creed – including his ascension.

This is not the place for an extended rebuttal of the 'demythologising' interpretation of so much in Scripture, but we do need to look more carefully at the ascension narrative. While mentioned throughout the New Testament, as we shall later see, the basic source for our information is in Luke's two volumes (Luke 24:50–53; Acts 1:9–11).

In these passages there is no trace of any hint that they were written as parables, much less a myth or legend. The author, a trained medical doctor, had gone out of his way to check the facts with first-hand eyewitnesses (Luke 1:1–4). In just three 'verses' covering the ascension (Acts 1:9–11), he mentions their physical sight of it five times ('before their very eyes ... from their sight ... looking intently up ... looking into the sky ... seen him go into heaven'). Such an account may be believed or disbelieved, but to treat it as fiction is to distort it beyond recognition.

We must return to the basic question: was it 'scientifically impossible'? This involves a closer look at what Scripture actually says and what science actually says.

The Bible does not commit us to a flat earth, around which the sun revolves. True, it uses 'phenomenal' language – that is, how things appear to the earth. To think that anyone who talks about the sun rising in the east and setting in the west must be a pre-Copernican ignoramus is ridiculous, any more than saying that 'the four corners of the earth' indicates belief in a square or cubed planet. Such everyday terms are intended to be pragmatic rather than scientific; they help with practical living rather than technical research (which requires specialist jargon).

The Bible uses the word 'heaven' in a more flexible way than many realise. In broad terms, it covers everything except planet earth; that is its meaning in both Genesis 1:1 and Revelation 21:1. The word can be used in the plural, referring to apparent 'layers', depending on the distance from the earth's surface. There are distinct 'heavens' in which the birds fly, the clouds form and the stars shine. Since the Creator is greater than all he has created, he must inhabit 'highest heaven', above all the others. This does not mean that he is far removed from the earth. He can take a walk in the Garden of Eden (Genesis 3:8). It is also true that 'in him we live and move and have our being' (Acts 17:28; Paul is quoting a pagan prophet with approval). He is Spirit and therefore is not locked into any particular 'place'. He can be anywhere he chooses to be (which is not the same as saying he is everywhere and is everything, an idea called 'pantheism', or 'in everything', called 'panentheism', both of which rule out hell as a place where God is not).

To ask: 'Where is God in the universe?' is therefore the wrong question, which can only get a wrong answer. 'Where is the universe in God?' would be more relevant. For if heaven is everything that is not planet earth, including whatever, if anything, lies beyond the universe, then heaven is all around us, as well as above us. And our Father in heaven is also around us.

But God is not the only inhabitant of 'heaven'. It is populated with hordes of heavenly beings, referred to in the Bible as angels. Also created by God, they are somewhat superior to human beings (Psalm 8:5) in appearance, strength and intelligence. Far from being empty of life, space is actually quite populated!

What does current science have to say about all this? Surprisingly, it is more sympathetic to the possibility than it used to be. Albert Einstein's theory of relativity and Max Planck's quantum theory have led to a radical change in understanding our space-time environment. It is now considered possible, though not probable, for two realities to occupy the same 'place', even for 'solid' bodies to pass through other 'solid' bodies existing in different 'dimensions' but the same location, invisible to each other.

In other words, the idea that heaven and space are co-terminous can no longer be ruled out on scientific grounds. But neither can this be demonstrated scientifically, much less proved. The methods and instruments used have so far found no trace of heaven – or God, for that matter. Science can

neither prove nor disprove the existence of either. Science has
its limits and is not necessarily the arbiter of all truth and
reality. The belief that it is (called 'scientism') is also a leap of
faith! Atheism requires as much faith as 'theism', which is
why scientists can be found in both positions.

But why has science completely failed to discover what we
may call this spiritual dimension of our universe? Precisely
because it *is* spiritual! God, for his own good reasons, has
chosen to hide himself and heaven from the prying eyes of
sceptics, seeking a voluntary response of trust and obedience
that has not been forced upon his creatures by incontro-
vertible evidence, leaving them no real choice.

But that does not mean that he himself and the heavens he
occupies are for ever beyond the reach of the physical senses
of humans, only that he reserves the right to control audible
or visible revelation. In Scripture, the classical case is that of
the prophet Elisha trapped by a besieging army in the town
of Dothan (2 Kings 6:15–17). His young companion despairs
at the sight of the surrounding enemy forces, but in response
to the prophet's prayer ('O Lord, open his eyes so that he may
see'), he saw, with his own eyes, the army of heaven all
around. Such glimpses of that 'other world' are scattered
through Scripture, but reach a climax in the New Testament
with Stephen (Acts 7:56), Paul (2 Corinthians 12:1–4) and
John (Revelation 4:1–11).

If heaven is so real, able to be seen by human eyes, and all
around us, is it interconnected with earth to the point where
travel between them is possible? Can a living being pass from
one to the other?

4

Is Heaven Open?

Given that natural and supernatural 'worlds' can co-exist, even in the same 'space', how open are they to each other?

Nature used to be regarded as a closed system, impervious to outside influence and entirely controlled by its own cast-iron laws. No miracles were possible. Natural effects could not have a supernatural cause. However, the discovery of random behaviour, even in atoms, has made the whole situation more flexible. The unexpected can happen, without apparent cause. The barrier between physical and meta-physical is not as solid as used to be thought and taught.

In the Bible, heaven and earth are clearly interconnected. Events in one affect events in the other (Revelation 12–13 is one example). The inhabitants of one can visit the other – and return.

From the first to the last book of the Bible, heavenly beings (angels) come to earth and play an important role in the affairs of men. They are heaven's messengers bringing tidings and taking back reports. They can assume human appearance (Genesis 18:2), consume and prepare food (1 Kings 19:5–7), even have sexual intercourse with women (Genesis 6:2; see also 2 Peter 2:4 and Jude 6).

They can freely move from one world to the other, as Jacob realised when he dreamt of a 'ladder' (more a two-way moving escalator is implied) 'reaching to heaven' (Genesis 28:12). They can transfer very swiftly, as Daniel discovered (Daniel 9:21–23); one had already shut the lions' mouths for him (Daniel 6:22). They can fly as well as walk, on earth as in heaven (Isaiah 6:2, 6).

Significantly, angels are on hand at the critical points of Jesus' life on earth – his conception in Mary's womb, his birth in Bethlehem, his temptations in the wilderness of Judea, his agony in Gethsemane, his resurrection from Joseph's tomb and his ascension to heaven (Luke 1:26–28; 2:8–15; Mark 1:13; Luke 22:43; 24:4; Acts 1:10–11). His crucifixion is a notable exception; even God was absenting himself (Mark 15:33–34).

Later, angels served the apostles, directing Philip to a meeting with an Ethiopian state treasurer (Acts 8:26–27), releasing Peter from prison (Acts 12:5–10), assuring Paul of his survival after shipwreck (Acts 27:23) and, above all, unveiling the future for John (angels are mentioned 50 times in the book of Revelation).

It is not an exaggeration to say that visits of heavenly beings to earth are an integral element in biblical history. They must be accepted, or rejected, with the rest of the record. But is heaven open to earth as obviously as earth is open to heaven? Can human beings visit heaven?

We are not asking where people go when they die. We have perhaps got too used to thinking of heaven in terms of an afterlife (even unbelievers tell children their grandmother has gone to heaven). Actually, in the Old Testament the dead were thought to have gone *down*, not up, to a world of disembodied and recumbent spirits (called *Sheol* in Hebrew and *Hades* in Greek). It was Jesus who brought the hope of going *up* to be with him in heaven, where he had already ascended himself.

We are asking whether any *living* human beings, still with breathing bodies, had ascended to that other world before Jesus. There are two possible cases.

Enoch is one. Scripture implies that he was one of the few, perhaps the only one, who lived a godly life in a godless society. Through a long life he 'walked with God' (Genesis 5:22). He had the courage not only to be different but also to rebuke the lifestyle of those around him, warning them that God would bring angels of judgement upon them (Jude 14–15 records his words). The flood in the days of his great-grandson Noah was the result. His reward for such loyalty was a unique ending to his life: '. . . he was no more, because God took him away' (Genesis 5:24). The language implies that he simply disappeared. 'Took' means he went to be with God (or the words would have been 'sent him away'). There was no body left behind to bury; he took it with him. But no one saw him go.

Elijah is the other. Like Enoch he lived a godly life himself and challenged the godlessness of his people. And he was also rewarded with a unique departure from this world. By contrast, someone saw him go. And he rode rather than walked. His apprentice and successor, Elisha, witnessed the unique event. They had been walking and talking by the River Jordan, on the opposite bank to Jericho, having just crossed over dry footed after Elijah had, like Moses and Joshua, divided the water. Suddenly, a 'heavenly' chariot drawn by horses charged between them, dividing them apart.

It is often wrongly assumed that Elijah was then scooped up into the chariot and carried to heaven. Actually, he 'went up to heaven in a whirlwind' (2 Kings 2:11). This would easily be enough to suck him away from the pull of gravity, though his cloak (with which he had struck the Jordan, causing it to dry up temporarily) was torn off, and fluttered to the ground at the feet of Elisha. There is a remarkable similarity to Luke's account of Jesus' ascension in the emphasis on an eyewitness testimony ('Elisha *saw* this. . . . And Elisha *saw* him no more').

However, the parallel with Jesus is far from complete. Both men went to heaven without dying and therefore with their original bodies, which were adapted to an earthly environment but not a heavenly one: '. . . flesh and blood cannot inherit the kingdom [or 'realm'] of God, nor does the perishable inherit the imperishable' (1 Corinthians 15:50). Bodies subject to age and decay would be totally inappropriate and useless in heaven.

We can only speculate about what happened to their old bodies. Probably they simply dissolved to nothing at a certain stage in their journey and both survived as disembodied spirits. Though in this form they could still visit earth and, like the angels, assume human appearance, as Elijah did centuries later (Mark 9:4).

So are people right when they claim that Enoch and Elijah are 'types', foreshadowing Jesus' ascension so much later? In one sense, yes. They demonstrate that heaven is open to human beings, though godliness is clearly a qualification.

In another sense, no. They did not die, nor were they raised again with a new 'glorious body', equally adapted to life in both worlds. They went with mortal, not immortal, bodies – and therefore as incomplete human beings.

It may even be that after their unique exit from this world

they rejoined the rest of the prophets, priests and kings in the waiting-room of departed spirits. Who knows?

What we do know is that Jesus categorically stated that: 'No-one has ever gone into heaven except the one who came from heaven – the Son of Man' (John 3:13, clearly referring to himself). He is claiming to be the first to do so, though very far from the last. His statement also points out the other huge difference between him and the two men we have been considering. He had come from heaven; they had not. He was returning to familiar territory; they were entering a new existence. He had been lower than he had ever been before; they were now higher than they had ever been. Or it may be that Jesus was referring to 'highest heaven', i.e. where God himself resided and no man had yet penetrated.

It is high time for us to look at his unique ascension to heaven.

5

What Exactly Happened?

There is less material in the New Testament covering the ascension than for any other major event during the Son of God's first visit to earth.

Take the four Gospels. Matthew does not mention it at all, probably because he was writing for new disciples who had already been told about it. Mark's Gospel, possibly embodying Peter's preaching, has lost its original ending: but the later completion contains the single phrase: 'he was taken up into heaven' (Mark 16:19). Luke's Gospel and his book of Acts, which bear all the marks of having been prepared as a legal brief for Paul's trial in Rome, give the most detail, since their recipient would be totally ignorant of what became of Jesus. John, written for believers of long standing, doesn't mention the ascension itself, but records Jesus' own prediction of it after the resurrection: 'I am returning to my Father and your Father, to my God and your God' (John 20:17; note 'returning' not 'going'). Few realise how different the Gospels are from each other – or why (for more information, see Volume I of my book *Unlocking the Bible:*

New Testament, Marshall Pickering 1999).

The Epistles, also written for believers, assume the fact of the ascension, without describing it. For Paul, the Lord Jesus Christ is 'the very one who ascended higher than all the heavens' (Ephesians 4:10), who was 'taken up in glory' (1 Timothy 3:16). For Peter, Jesus is the one 'who has gone into heaven' (1 Peter 3:22). For the anonymous author of the letter to the Hebrews, he has 'gone through the heavens' (Hebrews 4:14) and is now 'exalted above the heavens' (Hebrews 7:26). But from all these letters we learn nothing about the ascension itself, only what it led to.

Acts, which is the essential link between the Gospels and Epistles, contains the fullest description. Significantly, it is penned by the same doctor, Luke, who wrote the Gospel. This companion to Paul on his missionary journey wrote the legal brief for his friend's trial in two parts, the first ending with the ascension and the second beginning with it, providing literary as well as historical continuity. From the two records we have all the information we need about when, why, where and how it happened.

When? Jesus ascended to heaven exactly 40 days after he was raised from the dead. Since his resurrection was on the first day of the working week (our Sunday), his ascension was on the fifth day (our Thursday). His death 'coincided' with the Jewish feast of Passover (when the lamb was killed at 3 p.m. the day before) and his rising with the feast of Firstfruits (when the very beginning of the harvest was celebrated). His ascension was ten days before the feast of Pentecost (the completion of the harvest and celebration of the Law given to Moses at Sinai, which had led to the slaughter of three thousand), when the Spirit was given, which led to the salvation of three thousand.

Why? We are not at this stage asking what followed Jesus' ascension to justify his leaving earth (see Chapter 8 for that) but what preceded it, making it necessary for him to depart in the way he did. We can approach an answer by asking why he stayed around for approximately six weeks before finally leaving. What was he doing that needed that amount of time?

The first and most basic purpose was to convince the disciples that he had not just escaped death but conquered it once and for all; that he really was alive, more alive than ever, with a new and better body than the one they buried. This he did through many 'appearances' in different places and at different times (evenings in Jerusalem and Emmaus, mornings in Galilee). He offered 'convincing proofs' (Acts 1:3), inviting the disciples to touch his 'flesh and bones' (Luke 24:39), eating supper with them and cooking breakfast for them (Luke 24:41–43; John 21:9). At one point he 'appeared to more than five hundred of the brothers at the same time' (1 Corinthians 15:6), though some, perhaps on the fringe of the crowd, were not convinced (Matthew 28:17).

The second purpose was to give the disciples more teaching, especially what they would simply not have understood before. On the one hand, he gave them Bible studies, the first time he is recorded to have done this. From the three sections of the 'Old Testament' (the Law, the Prophets and the Psalms) he showed them how necessary and foreseen were his death and resurrection, his suffering being the way to his glory (Luke 24:27, 44–45). On the other hand, he had more to tell them about 'the kingdom of God' (Acts 1:3), especially its worldwide significance (note 'all nations' in Matthew 28:19; 'all the world' and 'all creation' in Mark 16:15; 'all nations' in Luke 24:47; 'the ends of the earth' in Acts 1:8). For the time being the universal dimension would have precedence over the national hope for the restoration of the kingdom to Israel, though that also would come in God's time (Acts 1:6–7).

The third and most significant purpose for our study was his need to prepare them for a very different relationship to himself. He had come back from the dead to be with them again, but not to stay. He had made this clear, even before he died (John 13:33), and certainly after he rose (his rebuke to Mary in the garden was not 'Don't touch me!' but: 'Do not hold on to me . . .' [John 20:17]).

The most extraordinary feature of those six weeks was not the appearances of the risen Jesus but his frequent disappearances, sometimes immediately after being recognised (Luke 24:31). In fact, he seems to have spent most of that period out of sight. Where was he when they didn't see him? Where did he go to? He didn't go back to *Hades* or go on to heaven, so he must have stayed somewhere on earth. Gradually it must have dawned on the disciples that he actually stayed with them all the time, wherever they were, in an invisible state. Thomas was probably the first to realise this, when Jesus revealed knowledge of his sceptical protest the previous week, even though he had apparently not been present – prompting Thomas to be the first human being ever to ascribe full divinity to this carpenter from Nazareth: 'My Lord and my God!' (John 20:28). Peter and Martha had previously recognised him as 'Son of God' (Matthew 16:16; John 11:27). But Thomas was the first to use the word 'God', unqualified, of the Nazareth carpenter. Later he carried this conviction to south India, where churches of 'Mar Thoma' exist to this day.

In other words, Jesus was preparing them for an intimate but invisible relationship. He was weaning them from dependence on their senses, necessary to prove he was alive, but useless after he ascended. There is a further aspect. Because he had a body, albeit a 'glorious' one (Philippians 3:21), he could not be in more than one place at once, whether visibly or invisibly. He could therefore only be with them all when they were together. But they would soon be scattered in all directions to be his witnesses. Yet he had promised to be with each of them 'always, to the very end of the age' (Matthew 28:20). Quite simply, had he stayed on earth in his risen body he could never have kept this promise.

Of course, we now understand that he would 'remain' with them by sending the Holy Spirit, so 'one' with him as to be virtually indistinguishable, a 'comforter' (the Greek word is literally 'stand by') he had promised to send in his place (John 14:16; 16:7). In a way, they already knew him, for he had already been 'with' them, working in Jesus himself; but he would be 'in' them, even closer than Jesus had been (John 14:17).

It was necessary for Jesus to go before the Spirit could come (John 16:7). The resurrection appearances could not therefore end with a final *disappearance,* as the others had done. The disciples might have concluded that he was still invisibly with them. There had to be a visible *departure* which convinced them that he himself had left the earth and returned to heaven (for a fuller discussion of all this, see my book *Explaining the Resurrection,* Sovereign World 1993).

That is why there had to be an ascension, following the resurrection, bringing Jesus' ministry on earth to a fitting conclusion. He had to go, and he had to be seen to go.

Where? From where did Jesus leave the earth? There is an apparent discrepancy between Luke's two accounts. One puts his departure in 'the vicinity of Bethany' (Luke 24:50); the other locates it on 'the Mount of Olives', a Sabbath day's walk (one thousand paces) from the city (Acts 1:12). The difference is resolved if he ascended from the eastern slopes of the mountain, between the village and the peak (and therefore not where two 'rival' churches have been built to commemorate the event!). This would be out of sight from the city and in tune with the absence of any resurrection appearance to other than believing followers.

How? Jesus did not raise himself, either from death or earth. He was 'raised' and 'taken up', literally 'carried' – in both cases by the agency and power of God himself. The text implies he rode up on a cloud (Psalm 104:3). If so, at a certain point the cloud beneath him would hide him from ground level.

He was standing upright, with arms extended forward, hands palm down. Palms up would have indicated prayer to the Father; palms down means blessing people (Luke 24:50). This posture was maintained as he steadily rose and until he disappeared into the clouds above. Clouds signify a westerly wind bringing moisture from the Mediterranean, but they also represent God's glory, the nearest thing in the natural world to his dazzling splendour.

Long after he had disappeared, the disciples were still gazing into the sky, hoping perhaps for one last distant glimpse. They hardly noticed two men in white clothes (the garb of angels) who had joined the small group, until they were addressed 'Men of Galilee'. The accuracy of this salutation is a tiny confirmation of the reliability of the record. All eleven disciples present were 'northerners' from Galilee; the only 'southerner' in the twelve had been Judas Iscariot (i.e. from Kerioth), who was now dead.

At first sight, the angels' message seems somewhat

contradictory: '. . . why do you stand here looking into the sky? This same Jesus, who has been taken from you into heaven, will come back in the same way you have seen him go into heaven' (Acts 1:11). Logically, we might have expected something like: 'Stop looking; he won't be back', or, 'Stop looking; you won't be seeing him again'. But, 'Stop looking because he's coming back down again' seems a little odd. Clearly, they are being discouraged from staying where they are and watching for his return. Obviously, he will not be returning for some considerable time, much less that day. They will not see him again in the immediate future. So they return to the city.

Such is the account of the event we call 'the ascension'. We now turn to the sequel, both on earth and in heaven.

6

How Did the Disciples React?

They had just said goodbye to their best friend. Jesus had come to mean everything to them. They had left their homes and jobs to travel with him for the last three years. They had lost him once already through death – and, to their utter amazement, had him back with them again after only three days, and for six whole weeks. But now he'd gone again, and this time they knew they would not see him again for what could be a long time.

The normal human reaction would be sadness, loneliness, even depression. Certainly nostalgia, looking back with a sense of loss.

Yet the disciples 'returned to Jerusalem with great joy' (Luke 24:52). It was as if they were celebrating his departure! This surprising response is yet another indication that the record is authentic; no one would have made that up. It is also evidence that this was no normal situation, primarily because the one they had seen off was no normal human being.

They were certain that the Jesus they had known was fully human. It would have been impossible not to have believed that after knowing him so intimately – walking the same roads, sailing in the same boat, eating at the same table, sleeping in the same room.

Now they were convinced that he was fully divine as well. He had hinted at this many times, not least in his use of the divine name 'I am' in statements about himself. He had done things only God himself could do: changed water into wine, raised the dead, calmed the storm and forgiven sins. There was plenty of evidence to support his claim to be the only and unique Son of God, his Father.

But the authorities had called him a liar, guilty of blasphemy, a sin deserving death in the Law of Moses (the charge was changed to treason, to secure his execution under Roman law). And God did not intervene in the trial, or the carrying out of the execution. The disciples must have had their faith in Jesus shattered by this dreadful miscarriage of justice and even asked how a good God could stand by and let it happen (Luke 24:21).

But God had intervened – three days later. He had reversed the verdict and the sentence. Far from being too bad to live, Jesus was too holy to be left to rot in a grave (Psalm 16:10, quoted by Peter at Pentecost, Acts 2:27). Far from telling lies about himself, he had told the truth. The resurrection proved that he was who he said he was (as Paul was later to realise, Romans 1:4).

The ascension was the final demonstration, if they needed it. As he went back up into the heaven he had come from, his disciples knew, beyond all shadow of doubt, that God himself had been with them in Jesus. In knowing the Son so well, they had also come to know the Father. They had been closer to God than anyone else had ever been! Their forefather Abraham had been the friend of God (James 2:23) but never like this. And they were just a bunch of ordinary men, who had earned their living with their hands.

Their sheer wonder at the privilege that had been theirs led, as it should, to worship. This part of the narrative seems to have escaped the notice of many, even those who think and talk about the ascension. After Jesus had disappeared and before they returned to Jerusalem, 'they worshipped him' (Luke 24:52). Thomas had already adored him as 'my Lord and my God' (John 20:28). Now all the eleven joined in praising the God-man, Christ Jesus. With uplifted hands and voices they extolled and glorified their risen, ascended Lord. Surely this was the best time of spontaneous and exuberant worship they had ever had.

Those of us who have been used to worshipping Jesus as Lord (even become too familiar with doing so, God forgive us) find it difficult to realise the full significance of this uninhibited praise. These were Jews, brought up under Jewish monotheism, the essence of which was to insist that there was only one person called God, and to use divine terms or titles of anyone else was the ultimate sacrilege. To do so was to run the risk of death. Yet they had no hesitation. It was the truth. It was the reality. God was God. Jesus was God. Father and Son were both God, equally to be praised and worshipped together.

Was this the heart of their 'joy'? Is this why they were so glad to see him go? Heaven was now where they wanted him to be, where he ought to be, where he belonged. That was where he could regain the glory that he once had, as they had overheard him pray on the night before he died (John 17:5). Who would want to keep him back, away from all that was rightly his? It was all so right and fitting.

And it meant that everything else was right, too.

Everything he'd said while on earth was true. Everything he'd done was necessary. Even his death on the cross was a triumph, not a tragedy. It was all as it should have been, clearly planned by God himself. Seen now in hindsight, the *past* looked utterly different.

So did the *future*. Jesus would be coming back. He'd promised to. And if they died before that, they would go to heaven to be with him all the sooner – and return with him when he came back to earth. Death had certainly lost its sting and the grave its victory (1 Corinthians 15:55, quoting Hosea 13:14).

And their *present* prospects were exhilarating. They were about to embark on a worldwide mission to tell everybody who would listen the thrilling news that God had loved the world so much that he had sent his only Son to live, die and rise again in it so that whoever goes on believing in him will never perish but go on having eternal life (John 3:16; the verbs are in the present continuous tense).

But they were to show, as well as tell, the good news, doing the miracles Jesus had done and even greater ones (John 14:12)! In a word, they were to continue all that Jesus 'began to do and to teach' (Acts 1:1) during his lifetime. In word and deed they would be his witnesses, testifying to his continued ministry.

They could hardly wait to get started, but they had to wait. Jesus had told them to. Their knowledge, experience and relationship with him were not enough to start, much less finish, the task he had given them (the same is true of us today, though we often try). They needed the same power that lay behind his own words and works. He promised to 'baptise' (literally 'plunge, soak, immerse') them in the same Spirit descending on himself at his baptism (Acts 1:5)

Surely they must have guessed it would be at Pentecost, just ten days ahead – all the major events so far had been on the high days of the Jewish calendar. When the festival came they were all in one place (the Temple, for the morning prayers at 9 a.m.), not just waiting but ready to obey the Lord's command to 'receive holy Spirit' after they heard him blow on them (John 20:22 describes the 'rehearsal' in the upper room; see my book *Jesus Baptises in One Holy Spirit*, Hodder and Stoughton 1998). By now they had been joined by over a hundred others and there would be three thousand more before the day was out.

For ten days they had not had the presence of Jesus or his Spirit. But they had each other and stayed together. And they spent much time talking to God, pouring out their gratitude for all he had done and their expectancy of all that he was going to do. It was his love that lay behind it all. Even prayer to God was now totally different. Since Jesus was their brother, they could address God as 'Father', even as 'Dad' (the nearest English equivalent of the intimate Hebrew *Abba*, which Jesus had used and encouraged them to use). And he had told them to use his own name in their prayer to ensure they got a positive response (John 14:14). Alas, this has often become a mere formula, but for them it expressed the confidence of having a friend in high places, the highest place, who had the ear of God himself – but a name to be used with care and consideration.

During this interim they had been joined by two other interesting groups. Women who had witnessed the resurrection but not the ascension came to pray with them. And Jesus' own family, his mother Mary and his four brothers, were also there. There had been a time when his brothers mocked his messianic pretensions (John 7:2–6) and even at one stage thought he had lost his mental balance and should be looked after (Mark 3:21). Now they knew how wrong they had been. Two, James and Jude, would later write parts of our New Testament. We don't know Mary's feelings; she was good at keeping things to herself (Luke 2:51). What we can say is that the sword that had pierced her soul (Luke 2:35) was now withdrawn and the wound was rapidly healing. Her unique role in the drama of our redemption had been beautifully fulfilled. John had taken the place of Jesus as her son (John 19:26–27). She is not mentioned again by name after Pentecost, but humbly took her place in the congregation of the church.

We have said enough to explain why the disciples had such 'great joy'. They had never been so happy in their whole lives: their entire outlook – past, present and future – had been transformed from deep pessimism to bounding optimism in just six weeks, from the resurrection of Jesus to his ascension.

And Jesus himself shared their exuberant feelings.

7

What Did It Mean to Jesus?

The public humiliation and prolonged agony of crucifixion were hard enough for any victim to bear. It was far worse for Jesus. During his final three hours he also suffered the darkness, thirst and loneliness of hell – the price of being made 'to be sin for us' (2 Corinthians 5:21). At his lowest ebb he cried out: 'My God, my God, why have you forsaken me?' (Mark 15:34, words recalled from Psalm 22:1).

What kept him going through this appalling time? We are told that it was 'for the joy set before him' that he 'endured the cross, scorning its shame' (Hebrews 12:2). It is no coincidence that this revelation is immediately followed by a reference to the ascension. This anticipated 'joy' centred on his return to heaven.

So when he went out of sight from his disciples, Jesus was as full of 'great joy' as they were. But for rather different reasons. And he had been looking forward to it much more than they had.

For one thing, he was going home. He had been away from his familiar surroundings for a third of a century. But 'home' is not just a place. It is where one is most loved and appreciated (that's what it should be on earth and always has been in heaven). Jesus was going home to be with his Father, his *Abba*, his 'Dad' – who had always loved him more than anyone else could.

He was coming home safe and sound. He had taken huge risks and faced great dangers, but he had come through them all. Now he was beyond the reach of all his enemies – Pharisees and Sadducees, Annas and Caiaphas, Herod and Pilate.

And he was coming home victorious, a conquering hero with a mission accomplished. He had taken on the devil and all his powers of darkness: 'And having disarmed the powers and authorities, he made a public spectacle of them, triumphing over them by the cross' (Colossians 2:15).

One can only begin to imagine the welcome he received in heaven from everyone there.

The saints of earlier days would have been excited. Moses and Elijah had already talked with him on the mountain of transfiguration 'about the exodus that he was about to accomplish at Jerusalem' (Luke 9:31, literally translated). Now they could welcome the liberator, not this time from slavery but from sin.

The angels who sang at his coming to earth must surely have done so when he returned to heaven. Now it would be 'Glory to Jesus in the Highest'. In fact, we have their new song in detail: 'Worthy is the Lamb, who was slain, to receive power and wealth and wisdom and strength and honour and glory and praise!' (Revelation 5:12).

Above all, a proud Father was at the centre of this celebration. If an earthly father could shower his love on a son who had wasted the family's resources and the best years of his life (Luke 15:20–24, surely representing God's love for sinners), how much, much more the heavenly Father would welcome a Son who had been to the far country without once yielding to its temptations, but maintaining his integrity – and never once having forgotten his Father. We may reverently guess what was said: 'Well done, good and faithful Son; enter into the joy of your Father'; and, to the saints and angels: 'This is my beloved Son, in whom I am well pleased; he was dead and is alive again.' Such service and sacrifice must now be rewarded.

At this point it will be helpful to take an analogy from the ancient world, which the New Testament writers also seem to have had in mind when describing the consequences of the ascension. It was not unknown for an emperor to appoint his son as the general of an army and send him to a distant part of the empire threatened by enemy forces. When these had been quelled, the son would return for a victory procession in his father's presence. He would lead the way at the head of his troops; these would be followed by captured prisoners in chains and, finally, by men carrying the spoils of war taken after the battle, to be distributed as gifts. As a reward, the emperor would invite his victorious son to share his throne, sitting at his right hand, the place of honour, to become his successor in the future, or co-regent, even his replacement, in the present. In the latter case, he would be crowned there and then. All this happened to Jesus at the ascension. Consider just one statement by Paul: 'When he ascended on high, he led captives in his train and gave gifts to men' (Ephesians 4:8, adapting words from Psalm 68:18). But the emphasis of the New Testament falls on the climax to the procession, when he 'sat down at the right hand of the Majesty in heaven' (Hebrews 1:3; *see also* 10:12).

This was the final destination of his ascension and is sometimes referred to as his 'exaltation', probably because of a key scripture (Philippians 2:5–11, a poem of six verses which may have been an early hymn). After describing the Son's self-humiliation, in choosing to become a human being, taking a serving role and accepting death by crucifixion, the passage goes on to say that 'therefore God exalted him' (verse 9, the verb is actually 'super-exalted' – that is, he could not have lifted him higher), and 'gave him the name that is above every name'. That name was 'Lord', and 'Jesus is Lord' became the earliest confession of faith in the church (1 Corinthians 12:3).

From another point of view, this climax to the ascension could also be called his 'coronation'. He was enthroned and is now 'crowned' (Hebrews 2:9). The crown of thorns he wore when he died has been replaced by a crown of gold (Revelation 14:14). He is now 'King of kings and Lord of lords' (Revelation 19:16), President of presidents, Prime Minister of prime ministers, Ruler of all rulers.

The ascension marks the beginning of his reign over the entire creation. 'All authority in heaven and on earth has been given to me' (Matthew 28:18). The carpenter of Nazareth is now King of the universe. This brings us to an essential, though often overlooked, feature of the ascension.

He was not the same as when he left heaven. Yes, it was the same Person. Yet he had changed, almost beyond recognition. He had left as a divine being. He was coming back as a human being. The angels saw a man, the Man, above them, for the very first time. They had to call him by a new name, his human name 'Jesus'. They had to get used to seeing him with a human body, though now shot through with the dazzling light of divine glory (as Peter, James and

John had once seen him, Mark 9:2–3; John 1:14; and Paul, Acts 9:3–5).

It cannot be emphasised too strongly that the 'incarnation' of God's Son was not just for 33 years, but for the rest of eternity. He was, is and always will be a human being, one of us, our brother (Hebrews 2:11). He did not discard his human nature when he ascended, but took it with him. How important this is for his present ministry we shall see in the next chapter. Meanwhile, let us meditate on two amazing implications.

First, there is a man in highest heaven. A member of our species is in the control room of the universe. No higher honour has ever been bestowed on the human race. No angel will ever be so exalted. God made us 'a little lower than the angels' (Psalm 8:5 AV); 'but we see Jesus, who was made a little lower than the angels' now far above them 'crowned with glory and honour' (Hebrews 2:9). But there is something even more astonishing than this.

Second, there is a man in God himself. Here is a mystery almost beyond the reach of our imagination. It was not just the Son who became human. Father, Son and Spirit are not just three 'persons'; they are 'one'. What happens to one profoundly affects the others, far more than the closest family. Jesus has taken our human nature into the 'Godhead' itself, not just into heaven. Humanity has become part of divinity.

One reason why we find this so difficult to grasp is that we have been far too influenced by Greek thinking about God as outside time and therefore beyond change. In Hebrew thinking, based as it is on God's revelation of himself, time is real to God. He is the God who was, is and is to come. Even God himself cannot change the past once it has happened, only the future. So there was a time when humanity was outside God; now it is inside God. There has been a radical change in God. God can never be the same again. Nor can we.

From the person and position of our ascended Lord, we turn now to his work in heaven on our behalf.

8

What Is He Doing?

Most Christians are well aware of what Jesus did for us while he was on earth: that he 'died for our sins according to the Scriptures, that he was buried, that he was raised on the third day according to the Scriptures' (1 Corinthians 15:3–4). But many are quite vague in their reply when asked what he has done for us since he went back to heaven.

Putting it another way, they are much clearer about his past than his present ministry. They think about and thank him much more for the former than the latter.

One reason for this imbalance could be the habit of preachers in referring to Christ's 'finished work' at Calvary, as if he there accomplished all that was needed for our salvation, which is simply not the case. True, he made a full 'atonement' for our sins, enabling them to be forgiven and us to be in a right relationship with a holy God, 'justified by faith' in his Son.

But that is far from being the whole of salvation. Indeed, the cross by itself could not take away sins (1 Corinthians 15:17). The resurrection is absolutely essential: 'how much more, having been reconciled, shall we be saved through his life!' (Romans 5:10). And the ascension is equally important to our salvation, since without it we could never have received the power to be saved from our sins themselves, not just their guilt but their power.

Jesus' post-ascension ministry is as vital to us as his pre-ascension work on our behalf. While this book is primarily about the ascension itself, it would be incomplete without a summary of the functions he is able to fulfil now that he is seated on the throne of heaven, at the right hand of God, his Father and ours.

He is not just our Saviour and Lord. He has been given over 250 names and titles in our Bibles – more than any other figure in history. And each highlights an attribute or activity relevant to our salvation. Some he earned while he was here on earth. Others have become his since his return to heaven. In this chapter we review a few of the latter.

The baptiser

There are two men called 'the baptist' in the New Testament: two cousins, John and Jesus. It was first applied to John, almost a nickname, describing what he was doing at the River Jordan, immersing people in the muddy water to wash away their sins, after they had both confessed them and demonstrated evidence of repentance. He was known as John the dipper, the plunger, the soaker – for that is what the word 'baptise' means in Greek.

But John could only get them clean, not keep them clean. He could deal with their past, not their future. For that they would need another 'baptiser', who would 'plunge' them into *holy* Spirit. He told his hearers about this repeatedly (Mark

1:7, the verb is in the continuous present tense, as it is in Acts 11:16 of Jesus' teaching).

So both John and Jesus majored on this 'soaking in Spirit' in their preaching and teaching. Yet Jesus never did it for anyone while he was on earth, either before or after his death and resurrection. He healed the sick, cast out demons, raised the dead, stilled the storm – all because he himself had received the Holy Spirit 'without limit' (John 3:34). But nobody else was as soaked or saturated in the Spirit as he was.

The truth was that no one else could be until he had returned to his heavenly home. Before the Spirit could come, he had to go (John 16:7). God had sent him from heaven. The Spirit had been sent from heaven to him after his baptism in water (Luke 3:21–22). He would need to return to heaven to claim the promised Spirit (Luke 24:49) from the Father before he could pour out the Spirit on others. 'Up to that time the Spirit had not been given, since Jesus had not yet been glorified' (John 7:39).

Significantly, this was the last thing Jesus spoke about before his ascension: 'For John baptised with water, but in a few days you will be baptised with the Holy Spirit . . . you will receive power' (Acts 1:5–8). And this was also the first thing he did after his ascension. As Peter said ten days later, at the feast of Pentecost: 'Exalted to the right hand of God, he has received from the Father the promised Holy Spirit and has poured out [i.e. from heaven] what you now see and hear' (Acts 2:33). The events at Pentecost were proof that Jesus had ascended into heaven itself, not just into the clouds.

This 'anointing' with power would enable the disciples to be, do and say what Jesus had been, done and said – to continue his mission in the world. And not just the 120 gathered in one place (the Temple, not an upper room) on that day. Pentecost was only the beginning. The ascended Lord went on pouring out his Spirit from heaven on others who repented, believed and were baptised (Acts 8:15–17; 10:44–46; 19:2–6). And he has continued to do so, right up to the present day. (For a thorough treatment of this whole subject, see the author's *Jesus Baptises in One Holy Spirit* and *The Normal Christian Birth*, both Hodder and Stoughton.)

The purpose of this 'Spirit baptism' is twofold. On the one hand, how could we ever live holy lives unless we were drenched with *holy* Spirit? Without such help, we'd swiftly drift back into our old ways and habits. But as we are 'led by' and 'walk in' the Spirit, he reproduces within us the character of Christ, growing the 'fruit' with nine flavours (Galatians 5:22–23).

But there are 'gifts' as well as fruit of the Spirit. 'When he ascended on high, he . . . gave gifts to men . . . some to be apostles, some to be prophets, some to be evangelists, and some to be pastors and teachers, to prepare God's people for works of service' (Ephesians 4:8–12). For others there will be a word of wisdom, a word of knowledge, gifts of special faith, healings or miracles, recognition of good and bad spirits, words of prophecy in an unknown language or translating it. In fact, it is the Lord's will that every believer have a gift to use in edifying the church and evangelising the world.

Obviously, it is impossible to be saved ourselves or help in saving others without this 'baptism'. It is no wonder that Jesus, who gave his disciples their huge task of taking the good news to the whole world before his ascension, warned them not even to attempt it until after he had ascended and asked his Father to send the Spirit to them.

He had confidence that the Father would give whatever he asked for, which brings us to his next ministry on our behalf in heaven.

The mediator

We sinners all need a priest to approach a holy God on our behalf. The Jews of the Old Testament understood this only too well. God himself had made it abundantly clear through the tabernacle in the wilderness and the Temple in Jerusalem that only qualified priests and supremely the High Priest were to enter his sanctuary, offering sacrifices and petitions for the people. Having lost the Temple, contemporary Jews have persuaded themselves they no longer need a priest, but they are mistaken.

Members of Orthodox, Catholic and high Anglican churches understand priesthood, since they use human beings for this function. Protestant Christians have rightly understood the New Testament teaching about the priesthood of all believers, each able to come to the throne of grace on his own behalf as well as others' (Hebrews 10:19–20). But they have often forgotten that they still need a High Priest in the presence of God himself. In Jesus we have such a one (Hebrews 9:12; 10:21).

His divinity qualifies him, and him alone, to represent God to us. But it is the humanity he took back to heaven when he ascended that uniquely qualifies him to be our ideal representative before God. Made in the likeness of sinful flesh, his own experience of temptation and suffering gives him sympathy when we face the same tests (look up Hebrews 2:18 and 4:14–16 right now).

We know that Jesus prayed for his followers when he was on earth (Luke 22:32). He still does, even though there are so many more in his heart now. 'Therefore he is able to save completely those who come to God through him, because he always lives to intercede for them' (Hebrews 7:25; Romans

8:34). When no one else is praying for you, he is.

'For there is one God and one mediator between God and men, the *man* Christ Jesus' (1 Timothy 2:5, my italics). There is only one – Christians need no other intermediary. To ask anyone else – saints, angels or even his mother Mary herself – to intervene on our behalf is to question his willingness or ability to speak for us. To insult God's high priest was serious enough for a Jew (Exodus 22:28; Acts 23:2–5); it is far more so for the Christian.

And how much we need him to speak for us, especially when we trip into sin. Every time this happens, it is debated in heaven! The devil hates Christians and delights to be 'the accuser of the brethren' day and night before our God (Revelation 12:10). He enjoys reminding God of his people's weakness and wilfulness. But we have an advocate, as well as an accuser, up there. 'But if anybody [i.e. a Christian] does sin, we have one who speaks to the Father in our defence' (1 John 2:1), provided we have confessed it in true repentance (1 John 1:9).

His mediation is necessary for our needs as well as our sins. His confidence in prayer to his 'Dad' may and must characterise our petitions also. Jesus said we would get what we ask for, provided we use his name and live by his words (John 14:13–14; 15:7). This is not just a magical formula to conclude a request and guarantee an answer. It means that it is a prayer Jesus himself *would* use in the circumstances and *will* pass on to his Father. It is a petition he can sign, adding his name to ours before it is presented to God.

How could we ever manage without such a High Priest to speak and act for us in highest heaven? But there's more.

The pioneer

Of all the titles Jesus has, this is one of the most interesting.

Again, it comes from the letter to the Hebrews (6:20). It is used of someone who goes ahead to blaze a trail for others to follow. He is the first of many, the individual vanguard of a multitude.

We have already seen that Jesus was the first human being to enter highest heaven and stay there. But not the last, by a very long way. He has opened up a way for others to follow. What is he 'pioneering' for us?

First, he is preparing a *place* for us. 'In my Father's house are many rooms . . . . I am going there to prepare a place for you' (John 14:2). He had shared in the creation of planet earth as a home for the human race. Later, he used the trees he had made, as a carpenter for 18 years, making doors and window frames, joists and rafters, helping to build homes and furniture for the inhabitants of Nazareth. Now he is building a city so big it would just fit inside our moon if it were hollow. And this 'new Jerusalem', erected in space, will come down out of heaven to be planted on the new earth (Revelation 21:2). No wonder 'no mind has conceived what God has prepared for those who love him' (1 Corinthians 2:9, quoting Isaiah 64:4).

Second, he is preparing a *position* for us. In the order of God's creatures, human beings were made a little lower than the heavenly beings, the angels (Psalm 8:5) and rather higher than the animals (Genesis 1:28). But this is not our final destiny in Christ, for we see Jesus, who was made a little lower than the angels [they looked down on him as they sang above Bethlehem], now crowned with glory and honour' (Hebrews 2:9): the angels looking up to him again, who is now a human being like us. And where he has gone we will follow.

Jesus may be the first human in highest heaven, but he will not be the last. We are to share his throne and reign with him – even over the angels! They will serve us as they have served the Lord.

This brings us to his supreme function as the ascended Lord.

The ruler

When Isaiah predicted Jesus' birth on earth, he added: '. . . the government will be on his shoulders' (Isaiah 9:6). And it now is.

Just before he ascended to heaven, Jesus announced: 'All authority in heaven and on earth has been given to me' (Matthew 28:18). He has qualified for this unique position by proving himself incorruptible by fame, wealth or power, humbling himself to the form of a slave and death on a cross (Philippians 2:6–8). He has proved himself capable of handling the highest office and responsibility with integrity.

First, he is ruling the *church*. The body is still on earth, but the head is in heaven. His mind, heart and will are communicated through what the Spirit says and what the Scripture has said. He knows all that goes on in every local fellowship. His letters to the seven churches of Asia (Revelation 2–3) reveal his style of government. He encourages what is good, rebukes what is not, chastises those he loves, even closes churches down when their light fades, holds out rewards and punishments, reminds them of his efficiency and sufficiency, feels happy or sad for them.

Second, he is ruling the *world*. Nothing happens that is not planned or permitted by him. And events are being shaped and over-ruled for the sake of his own followers. 'God placed all things under his feet and appointed him to be head over everything for the church' (Ephesians 1:22). So history is not out of control, contrary to all appearances. History is his story, and he is writing it.

Third, he is ruling the *universe*. Sun, moon and stars are all under his control and depend on the person who is 'sustaining all things by his powerful word' (Hebrews 1:3, describing the Son rather than the Father). There is a human being in the control room of the universe – our Jesus. If scientists reaching out into space realised or remembered this, they might be a little more humble. Nor would Christians be subject to ridicule and contempt. They are friends of the man at the very top!

The ultimate objective of his reign is clear: 'to bring all things in heaven and on earth together under one head, even Christ' (Ephesians 1:10). Then it really will be a *uni*verse, with every part operating in perfect harmony with all others.

There are, however, still many rebels refusing to acknowledge his lordship, even though they are already under it. That he has not banished them from his domain already is an expression of his love and compassion, wanting to give all ample opportunity for voluntary submission. But there will come a day when his patience is exhausted. If their hostility has persisted, he will then deal with them, as every good ruler must.

There is one verse in the Old Testament that is quoted more frequently in the New than any other – over 20 times – by Jesus himself and the apostolic writers (Matthew 22:44; 26:64; Mark 12:36; 14:62; 16:19; Luke 20:42f.; Acts 2:34; 5:31; 7:55; Romans 8:34; 1 Corinthians 15:25; Ephesians 1:20; Colossians 3:1; Hebrews 1:3; 5:6; 6:20; 7:17, 21; 8:1; 10:12f.; 1 Peter 3:22; Revelation 3:21). The verse is Psalm 110:1 – 'The Lord says to my Lord: "Sit at my right hand until I make your enemies a footstool for your feet." '

This was clearly the most fundamental thought about the Lord Jesus Christ in the minds of the early Christians – that he was seated on the throne of heaven. They did not think of him hanging on the cross, or even risen from the tomb: both were vital for salvation, but they were past events, to be remembered with gratitude. Their faith was kept up to date: they worshipped the ascended Lord, which is what he was to them then and still is to us now. He is neither on the cross nor outside the tomb. He is seated at the right hand of his Father in heaven.

Yet many professing Christians seem hardly aware of his present position. Why is this?

9

Where Is He Now?

The title of this chapter may come as a surprise to the reader. Surely such a question is quite superfluous after all that has been said so far.

Isn't the answer obvious? Our Lord Jesus Christ is seated at the right hand of his Father in heaven, having ascended there after his time here on earth.

Most Christians would probably give this answer if challenged with the question. However, what we profess with our lips is not always the same as what we practise in our lives. It is one thing to recite a creed and quite another to allow our beliefs to influence our hearts and minds.

We have already noted the general neglect of the ascension, and the tendency of Western churches, Catholic and Protestant, to focus their gospel on the dying rather than the living Christ – not so much an over-emphasis on the crucifixion as an under-emphasis on the resurrection. All this tends to make us think more about where he was then (on earth) than where he is now (in heaven); on what he did for us then than what he is doing for us now.

And there is an added complication, even when stressing that he is alive today. Many believers have picked up a strong impression that he is living *within* them now – and therefore is still down here. For all practical purposes they think of him as with them on earth, rather than with the Father in heaven.

The problem begins with the careless talk of enthusiastic evangelists. Whether appealing to crowds or individuals, they urge listeners: 'Invite Jesus into your life', or 'Receive Jesus as your Saviour', regardless of the absence of such calls in the New Testament. A recent large outreach in England crusaded under the banner 'J.I.M.', which stood for 'Jesus In Me'. The most widely abused text in the New Testament is Revelation 3:20 ('Behold, I stand at the door and knock. . .' AV); this verse has nothing to do with conversion, is addressed to backsliding believers and the 'door' is of the church, not the heart. Actually, it is the sinner who needs to knock for admission to the kingdom, and it is Jesus who opens the door – in fact, he *is* the door (John 10:7). As for 'receiving' Jesus, this was possible when he came to earth and he could be welcomed or turned away (John 1:11–12, note the past tenses of the verbs). But after the heavens 'received' him, the verb 'receive' was transferred to the person who has taken his place on earth. From Pentecost onwards, apostolic preaching called for repenting towards God, believing in the Lord Jesus and receiving the Spirit (Acts 2:38). The modern habit of running these three into one ('Receive Jesus') is quite misleading, not least because repentance of sin and reception of the Spirit can be overlooked (for a much fuller critique of this weakness, see my book, *The Normal Christian Birth*, Hodder and Stoughton 1989).

But are there not scriptures that talk about Christ living 'in' us? Yes, there are a few. Typical is: '. . . Christ in you, the hope of glory' (Colossians 1:27). But 'you' is in the plural and refers to the corporate body rather than the individual – in all of you rather than in each of you. This is very much in line with his promise to be in the midst where two or three are gathered together (Matthew 18:20 AV). The same applies to 'the kingdom of God is within you' (Luke 17:21, better translated as 'among you'; 2 Corinthians 13:5 is similar).

There is one 'proof-text' more quoted in this connection than any other: Paul's testimony that 'I have been crucified with Christ and I no longer live, but Christ lives in me' (Galatians 2:20). Nothing in this statement can be taken literally, i.e. physically. Paul had not been literally crucified, nor was it literally true that he no longer lived (in the very next sentence he begins: 'The life I live . . .'). And Jesus was not literally living inside him. What was true was that his old life had been put to death and, by the indwelling Spirit, the character and behaviour of Christ was being reproduced in his new life. Paul takes it for granted that his readers will understand that 'Christ lives in me' is the same as saying 'his Spirit is in me', which is his usual expression.

For the Spirit is the 'Spirit of Christ' and the 'Spirit of God' (Romans 8:9). When we receive the Spirit, there is a sense in which the Father and the Son also take up residence (John 14:23). This makes our bodies temples of the Spirit (1 Corinthians 6:19), temples of God (1 Corinthians 3:16) and members of Christ (1 Corinthians 6:15). Father, Son and Spirit are three persons who can be thought of separately, but they are so 'one' that they are all involved in each other's activity.

Nevertheless, they are clearly differentiated in Scripture. The New Testament mainly talks about the Spirit in us, less frequently about us in him. Occasionally it speaks of Christ in us, but far more often we are said to be 'in Christ'. The difference of emphasis is very important.

Since the main emphasis is on Christ above us in heaven, rather than within us on earth, there are some far-reaching implications.

For one thing, our thinking will have a new centre of gravity, pulling our minds up to heaven just as our bodies are pulled down to earth. Christians have often been ridiculed for being 'so heavenly minded they are no earthly use'. The element of truth in the jibe is that they can be concentrating so much on the future that they neglect the present. But the opposite is probably the real truth, especially in the contemporary church. We can be so earthly minded that we are no heavenly use! With minds saturated with media and advertising junk, we find it next to impossible to rise above the level of living all around us, and find ourselves as worldly-minded as everyone else.

The antidote is simple: '. . . set your hearts on things above, *where Christ* is seated at the right hand of God. Set your minds on things above, not on earthly things' (Colossians 3:1–2). If it is true that 'as . . . [a man] thinks within himself, so he is' (Proverbs 23:7), here is one of the great secrets of successful Christian living. It is not hard to let the mind frequently drift to where a loved one is. And if we think of the Lord we love in heaven, our mind's reflections and heart's ambitions will focus more on the joys there than the pleasures here, the virtues there than the vices here, the rewards there than the restrictions here.

Ask yourself a simple question: 'What have I set my heart on having, and where is it – on earth, or in heaven?'

But there is more to it than a refocusing of mind and heart. This is only possible when certain things have already happened to our spirits. The statement quoted above from Paul's letter actually begins: 'Since, then, you have been raised with Christ' (Colossians 3:1). A little earlier he has already said: 'Since you died with Christ' (Colossians 2:20).

A Christian is someone who is 'in Christ' rather than someone who has Christ in them. The latter makes him 'smaller' than us, but he is 'greater'. And being 'in' him means that our spirits have actually shared in those historical events through which he 'pioneered' our salvation. We have been crucified with him in a real though not a literal sense; our 'old self' is dead and gone. We have been raised with him. And we have ascended with him.

If Christ is in heaven and I am in Christ, then I am in heaven, too. 'And God raised us up with Christ and seated us with him in the heavenly realms in Christ Jesus' (Ephesians 2:6; note that 'raised' includes both resurrection and ascension). That is my real position, where my spirit now is. 'For you died, and your life is now hidden with Christ in God' (Colossians 3:3).

Of course, our physical senses tell us that we are down here on earth, and our minds will believe only what our bodies tell us – unless we exercise our faith by regularly reminding ourselves that we are 'in' the ascended Christ. Death will resolve the tension in a moment. Christians don't 'go to heaven' when they die. They are already there! Just as soon as the body stops telling them they are on earth, their spirits will tell them they are in heaven – where their real life has been 'hidden', from their own and others' physical senses, ever since they came to be in Christ. There will be no long journey through space or time. It will be like dropping off to sleep and waking up a moment later in the presence of Jesus. No wonder Paul said: 'I desire to depart and be with Christ, which is better by far' (Philippians 1:23).

That would be a lovely note on which to conclude this little book. But that cannot be the end of the story of the ascension, with Jesus and ourselves in heaven. Neither he nor we will be staying there; heaven is only a waiting-room.

10

Will He Stay There?

At the ascension itself, the two angels told Jesus' disciples about a future 'descent' from heaven. As he had gone back up to heaven, so he would be coming back down to earth.

He will come back as 'this same Jesus' (Acts 1:11), the same person they had seen go. He would not have changed in the meanwhile. He would still be human, with a real body that could cook and eat food, but no 'older'. Since the resurrection, 'Jesus Christ is the same yesterday and today and for ever' (Hebrews 13:8) – in every way.

He will come back 'in the same way you have seen him go' (Acts 1:11). Had the disciples been able to make a film or video record of the ascension and we played it backwards, we could watch his second coming on the screen. Down through the clouds, nearer and nearer – except that this time his disciples on earth, thousands and thousands of them, will meet him up in the air (1 Thessalonians 4:17), giving them all a better chance to see and welcome him. And he will be accompanied by myriads of angels (who will be blowing trumpets) and all the saints who have already died (1 Thessalonians 4:14), among them my grandfather, who ordered his tombstone to be engraved with the words: 'What a meeting!' It will be the biggest, noisiest Christian meeting ever held, up in the air because no stadium on earth could hold the crowd.

He will come back to the same place. Since he will be in his human body, it can only be one place, and it will be the spot from which he left – the Mount of Olives (Zechariah 14:4). All disciples still alive on earth are promised a free flight to the Holy Land for the big event, accompanied by angels (Matthew 24:31), leaving unbelievers behind, even close relatives and friends (Matthew 25:40–41), and finding on arrival that they and all the others have brand new bodies, just like Jesus' glorious body (1 Corinthians 15:51–52; Philippians 3:21).

When will he descend again? How long will he stay on his second visit to our planet? Will there be a second 'ascension'? Above all, why does he need to come back? And why bring all the saints in heaven back to their former residence? Such questions as these are not relevant to the scope of this study, and I have tried to answer them elsewhere (*Explaining the Second Coming*, Sovereign World 1993 and the much fuller *When Jesus Returns*, Hodder and Stoughton 1995).

I have only mentioned this because there is a direct connection between his departure from earth and his return to earth. Neglect of the one invariably leads to an indifference to the other. When his ascension to reign in heaven is ignored, his return to reign on earth is no longer at the heart of Christian hope for the future. A bishop recently interviewed on BBC radio was asked if he believed in the second coming of Christ to earth and replied: 'No, because he never went away.' Enough said!

The opposite is also true. Those who constantly look to the

Lord *in* heaven confidently look for the Lord *from* heaven. They 'wait for the blessed hope – the glorious appearing of our great God and Saviour, Jesus Christ' (Titus 2:13). They long for his appearing (2 Timothy 4:8). Their prayer is: 'Come, Lord Jesus' (Revelation 22:20).

May it be soon!